The Book of Revelations

Sophie Léone

www.iamsophieleone.com

Wise Lioness Publishing, Suffolk, UK

ISBN-13: 978-1-7399509-0-3 print edition

Cover Art by SOPHIE
Prints: lovesophieart@icloud.com

Cover Design by Shaun Lubbock

Write what you wish.

CONTENTS

4: "We turn from the inside"

5: "I haven't lost my mind. I've gained my soul"

INTRODUCTION

by Violette Beauregard

(world-renowned authority on art speaking to truth through satire and absolutely nothing to do with Roald Dahl)

When Sophie Leone approached me to write the foreword to her first book *The Book of Revelations*, my whole being resounded with a capital YES, without having read a single word.

Having regaled many hours in her company, I knew in an instant the moment she decided she was ready to publish was the moment our world would receive an ally in the field of encouraging itself to feel and to express in the way that humanity was intended: freely and unshackled.

It is my pleasure to introduce the vivacious, curious and gloriously eye glinting Sophie Léone, a wise lioness soul whose magnetic energy attracts and retains attention. Her words, her voice, simply MAKE SENSE.

In her is something deeply feminine and holding. She speaks truth and has no hidden agenda. You feel safe around her.

Her truth can feel like the sharp blade of a knife; you cringe a bit, you resist a bit, but something about the timbre of her voice makes you TAKE NOTICE. She knows you. She's met you before and she is a shrewd judge of character.

She knows how to take you on a journey through her stories. When you listen, all of your senses come alive.

She is cream puffs and poetry, a glass of red wine in front of a roaring fire. She's the feathers in the duvet. Tender and vital, her discernment is SHARP.

Not one to mess with, she assumes nothing, believes no one and challenges everything.

She is here in peace. Her desire: to make you feel SOMETHING.

Her power is in her KNOWING; she knows instantly whether something is for her or not. She cares not one iota the rest of the world operates in linear lines; she is WOMAN and a fierce stand for HUMANITY and CHILDREN.

Her integrity is GOLD. She trusts the messages received from spirit. With her finely tuned ear for language and meaning, she translates them with ease.

As a double agent, she works inspiring souls to feel in the daytime AND the night time. She is the friend of the darkness, the glint in her eye a clue as to her knowing of the dark's secrets.

She knows it's all a game. She loves to play.

Her forte is acting, improvising, finding doorways in and out and all the way through. The original Passe-Partout, she floats through situations wielding a layer cake of wit, humour, charm and hypnotic fluid eloquence.

She says what is on the tip of your tongue. Watching her move to music and hearing her sing from the depths of her tantalising sacral sways is like rediscovering the reason why you are alive.

Stealthily, she digests what she sees and feels, then regurgitates the bones for you.

The bones for you to rebuild your spine and reconstruct humanity based on the economy of the heart.

She makes an extortionately extravagant conscious living receiving offers for her voice, her words and her presence. She speaks, she writes and sometimes, she holds gatherings for free, open-hearted humans stepping into the evolution of their consciousness.

I should know. I am She.

Welcome to the book opening you up to your own marvel.

AUTHOR'S PREFACE

It is the norm to be held

to take time to be

to laugh, to write, to sing

to tune in

to feel empowered in your own skin and bones

to dance to YOUR OWN TUNE.

This is the BACKBONE we are re-building.

My name is Sophie. I strongly dislike reducing myself into words to describe what I ‘do’.

For the purpose of this endeavour, I can say to you one constant has been my love for observing life around me and writing about it.

Simply, I document these treasures and translate their wisdoms into stories which activate a remembering in humans on the ground.

Part memoir, poetry, dream visions, short story and infused with spells, *The Book of Revelations* is an intimate, complex and major investigation into the essence of our purpose.

It’s about having the courage to go to the edge and leap, to question the conventional in search of other worlds, the truth of embodying the majesty of being a soul in a human body and all the different realms we have the power to delve into.

The Book of Revelations is a treasure trove of the unpicking and piecing together of a mother’s mind.

It will remind, comfort, confront and console you. Each page reveals an excavation of ancient hidden clues to heal, bringing our ‘classified’ demons out from the under belly of shame and vulnerability.

Written and weaved with the true eye of a keen observer, the 70 stories are an alchemy of soul, imagination, nature and parallel worlds. They rainbow arch the beauty and gifts open to us at any given time, whether we are ready to receive them or not.

The timing of the words is as potent as the prophecies held within, exposing the deep truth of taking radical self-responsibility.

My wish is to leave you feeling inspired to believe you are capable of going for your dream and feel all the goosebumps you deserve to feel during your lifetime here on Earth.

This is our collective moment. It's time to lead by example.

As a preface to this adventure, you need to know you are exactly where you need to be in this moment and there is nothing else to be done.

Trust this is what you need right now.

As a first practice, you are invited to settle down.

Set aside everything you think you know about what a book should look like and contain.

We evolve by getting out of our heads and diving deeply into our hearts. Prepare to be touched and moved.

Take three deep breaths, connect with your heart and ask your deep wisdom what you need to hear today.

Just as you would with a deck of tarot cards, flick through your book and allow your soul to speak through the page you chose. Allow her to speak to you as if you were sitting next to her on a park bench or on the grass, chatting.

You are of course free to choose YOUR way. Read from front to back or back to front (no one ever read The Bible all the way through, did they? These here Revelations are no different).

Thank you so much for being here, reading the dream I am living and made happen.

This is my story, and yours.

EnJOY

Sophie xxx

Our collective strength nourishes us.
We value our creations.
We are the sovereign, sacred children of Mother Earth.

Part 1

"When you de-institutionalise, there is no system"

EULOGY TO MY WARRANT CARD

You were my identity
my special pass to powers
a badge of honour
full of pride
and worship
and desire

I carried you with me 15 years
on duty and even off

I loved you until I began to question you
or was I questioning me?
Who felt no longer fit to serve?
Was it you or was it me?

The conditions restricting my every sense
the handcuff holder torn

The oath of office heavy on a girl
who already
had her own powers and authority
outside of the warrant to affirm.

15 years into 15 minutes for a eulogy to you
seems hardly fitting yet strangely, I feel satisfied
so here's my heartfelt thanks to you.

Rest in Peace Detective Sergeant 1341 Sophie Léone,
You are reincarnated.

CAUTION: YOU DO NOT HAVE TO SAY ANYTHING

(a knuckle rap on institutions)

Can we police without EGO?

I will always be a detective in my heart.

There's a reason my calling took me there early in my service.

I care so much. I value the role of policing so much.

Hence,

I want to kick the arse out of an institution that can do SO MUCH BETTER.

I WILL emote and speak and ask poignant questions.

It burns me up when I see incompetence and disdain.

I don't care for which systems you want to use. I want things done properly.

I am a moral person.

I'm here to serve.

I'm here to learn.

It's been my world.

I've stared deeply into the eyes of people who have raped and have been raped.

I've stood on the front line when we didn't need to be there.

I've been cockblocked, treated unfairly, worked with officers with no desire to be there anymore.

I've had the best and the worst times.

We are not valued. You do not value us.

I'm not finished.

We are here to serve. We know the toil, the deal, it's what we are here to do.

How dare we treat valuable officers the way we do?

Don't fuck me over and tell me it's about the right or wrong thing when all you want is to get to the next rung of your ladder and pander to someone else's political agenda.

Why can't we admit when we are wrong or make a shit decision?

Why do we routinely post zombies into key roles with no leadership skills?

To lead is to give hope.

To be honest.

To listen.

To call bullshit when it is seen.

To not fear what others think.

To not give in to intimidating tactics.

To be soft and strong at the same time.

To be fierce, authoritative, clear, inspiring, endearing, trustworthy.

I dare to stand and make a change.

To be the change.

My experience matters.

My experience as a police officer has meaning and value.

My experience as a human being has meaning and value.

There is always a sacred human being behind the number.

I’m now going to caution you:

You do not have to say anything,

BUT

it may fog your soul if you do not reflect,

when questioned, on something which will shape your grandchildren’s futures.

And anything you do or say or think or write, in this now moment, has the capacity to make either your best dreams or worst fears come true.

Do you understand?

HUMANS AND CHANGE

Humans allow the ego to be in charge.

Ego; ergo, the head - the personality which, while it gives humans spice, believes it's the boss. It isn't. The heart is. If only humans would give their heads a break and trust the other engine has got them; the key to change is right there.

Humans have spent so long conditioned within their constricted, restricted institutions, that even though they are expert detectives, qualified to the hilt nurses, surgeons, teachers, heads of industry or nations: they are blinded by the box they are locked in by.

They have lost the ability to think critically or for themselves. They've been in the system so long, that to leave and live differently is unimaginable, the thought of it reduced to the realm of fantasy once a few wines have been consumed. The one-night stand dream tinting the cheeks rosy, then wake up, all gone.

Back in the box. Back to never daring to go or question beyond.

Whether it's a conscious decision or not, there's a stubbornness in wanting to believe there is no way the institutions would ever get things so wrong, even though, humans have personal experience of that fact.

They have evidence of treatment upon themselves or witnessed it on others, and have felt the plethora of sadness, anger, anxiety and incompetence. The history books are full of such accounts.

Humans will tell themselves this is the way it is. That at least they get paid. They will say things like 'what doesn't kill you makes you stronger'.

Indeed, humans will reinforce that belief by looking around them at the myriad of others in the same life system and reason 'if so many humans are still in it, surely it can't be that bad'.

Fear is driving the system. Humans are fearful of travelling sober to the edges of their world and get across the big void in front of them staring them in the face. The void of faith. They choose not to take the leap. They don't want to make a mistake.

Yet, it's that mistake, that risk, that 'taking a pun' with change which gives humans LIFE.

IF ONLY

If only we were
        slow enough
        to feel enough
To feel ourselves
        as we are
        powerful as we are
        resplendent as we are
AS I SEE YOU
x

THIS HERE LAND IS OUR PLAYGROUND

What if we ended up spending less on fuel getting to jobs we don't enjoy?

What if we ended up wearing the clothes we actually want to wear and not spend money on tight suits and shoes making us less able to move freely within our bodies?

What if once we've extricated ourselves from the need to BE the teacher, the lawyer, the accountant, the head of marketing, we allow ourselves to pick up our pencils or paint or sit down or dance or play the piano?

What if we let go of this absolute NEED TO CONTROL everything in our lives and others'?

What if we allowed ourselves to choose OUR path?

What if in doing so, for the first time, we get to feel a different kind of vibe, and the currency by which we trade our lives becomes sacred?

What if this opens up space?

What happens when we feel into that space and relax our limbs?

What if we went easy on ourselves?

Would the world crumble if the six pack was less defined? If the toaster and kettle didn't match?

What if you were more resourceful than you know?

What if this KNOWING actually gave you fresh lungs and wings?

What kind of foothold do you need to get yourself there?

Give yourself a break. A load of your old rules will soon no longer apply. Trust.

Welcome home. To your home. Your new playground.

THE RICHES OF DIVERSITY

People are rich in experience- just like you are, and when you take the time to HEAR THE STORY, magic happens; something opens up.

Growing up, I wanted to 'be' many things: detective, beautician, actress, tv presenter, journalist, PR or something involving French.

There was a suggestion I could be an interpreter, but I wanted to speak for ME, not rehash someone else's words.

Maybe I knew it right there in that moment: forget the label, whatever I end up doing or being, it has to be from me.

I SPEAK FOR MYSELF. I trust that because I'm so connected to this at source, I also speak YOUR language. We all have the capacity to hear each other and choose.

I come from a multi-national family, raised in the south of France amongst a melting pot of languages and ethnicities. I've always revelled in the intricacies of language. Viewing both sides. Communication. The why of things.

When we share our knowledge, our hearts, our experiences, we raise our game. When we do this from a place of FREE CHOICE and INTEGRITY and LOVE, the connections we make are worth everything.

Knowing other ways helps unite us, think outside of the box, and affirm which way feels right for us deep within.

We all have a story. We all have value. We add value.

Be aware of what is being silenced. Wonder why.

If you don’t hear or see it, it will appear not to exist and yet...

It’s there and just as valuable.

CAUGHT FREE

There you were, with your noise and
hustle of the morning rush
still here, after all these years.

Your chain link fence
and CCTV cameras
around you.

That's when it struck me.
I wasn't inside anymore.
You were.

I was FREE.

SUITCASE WEAVERS

Members of a television production company were gathered around and within the edges of a giant suitcase, the stitching of which was fragile, damaged and compromised. They were bursting at the seams. The situation was dire.

They looked at one another, each one an inherent part of the fabric of this dishevelling. They knew each had to desperately keep threading to keep it together. This was not their first time. They also knew this would cause each other deep pain as they once again jabbed the needle into their fellow humans' flesh, the fabric of their world.

An older, wise woman hovered nearby. She was free from their shackles and offered an alternative way.

Her approach was seeded from a different root to theirs. It was not what they had been taught to know their whole lives and yet they KNEW, as they felt the deep collective stirring of her presence, it was now time to release.

Mysteriously and meticulously, she danced as she weaved the thread up and over and through the fabric avoiding each person, holding them rock steady as they moved over and under, as the waves of the weave shook them from their cells.

Finally, with the most exquisite orchestration of a swift flick of the wrist, the wise woman pulled the thread within, closing up the wound, shining the light of golden stitches, providing the same relief they had felt during the rare moments they had happened to find themselves in the grace of unadulterated communion with the stars.

The path was now lit.

Part 2

"This is an 'Emerge and See' Situation"

INVOCATION

I invoke

the spirit of the owl to partner with me,

the power of the ancient woman and the Earth,

the hag, Odin stone and all her through ways for us to see,

the softness and the warmth of nature's wool to hold us while we come through.

I take up my space to read between my lines. I see and feel everything.

People see fortune tellers.

I'm a truth teller who has spent years dealing with people and smelling bullshit.

I call it out.

Through my reams of dreams and access to the powers of the darkness under closed eyelids, I have insight. I see your secrets and your truth through a myriad of ways and tunnels.

I am a gateway for you to step in and out of your mind. I make portals and possibilities appear in front of your eyes. I see you through your eyes, your voice, your writing.

I am a soul translator. A conduit from Earth to Spirit. A writer, a creator of worlds.

I tell the truth, the whole truth and nothing but the truth.

No filters. I'm here to make you feel.

For when you feel, you change the world. Truth.

PATRIARCHY'S ARK

We are all housed within a boat on a massive ocean.

There are steam rooms, restaurants and all the mod cons.

Within this vessel, the fissures are repeatedly superficially plastered over.

We and our babies are being carried and held

at the mercy of the architects of this ark.

Except, whose mercy? Who made the architects?

The fissures are cracking with questions thirsty for truth.

We are at Her mercy. Not this vessel's.

The big body of water. The waves. The huge waves.

We rock and balance upon her at her whim.

She.

In a night of nauseous darkness, I peeked out. I had to witness.

I saw Her might, foaming, navy, high and CRASHING.

I held my breath and looked into her for the first time.

I saw Her. A light form of pinkie red.

A jewel at the centre of the crashing tempest.

I saw Her.

She was mad.

Not mad bonkers.

Mad angry.

The Mothership was back.

FEEL BEFORE YOU SPEAK

Whatever your experience of this powerful moment in your lifetime, I hope it brought you to your knees at least once. That moment of deep loss; whatever that represents for you, where there is no option but to meet it, because it is in those deep feeling moments that a gateway of choice opens.

I hope you allowed yourself to release into the discomfort. Yes, it's an inevitable sucker punch unbearable door to discernment. It helps you to KNOW for absolute certain what matters to YOU INSIDE. Not your best friend, or #influencermum with all the followers.

It's your choice and opportunity to make a change from here on in, whatever sphere of life. This applies to everything.

An opportunity to look in the mirror at your preconceived ideas and to feel into what it is that actually triggered you into the thought, the reaction. That reaction that makes you unleash it all in that split second.

Truth bomb: you literally do not have to say anything.

Can you sit in the pause and digest your feelings instead?

Either way, know there is only one way for you, and this is YOUR WAY.

It's you getting off the merry go round of relying on everyone else's (re)actions and opinions in order to determine yours.

No matter how long it takes you, make the time to feel into your pain, your discomfort, your joy, your wobbly spots and go into your HEART, your BODY. YOUR KNOWING WHAT'S RIGHT AND CONGRUENT WITHIN YOU.

This, my dear friends, is YOUR TRUTH. This is your way to effective, loving change for you and everyone else around. They may not like this new you, because you will stop doing the stuff you don't need to do anymore. So yes, it's scary.

The world really needs you to come down from your head. Look at the shit we're in. Time for something new.

Feel before you speak.

THE END

I keep roaming to the various spaces of the land and getting to the edge.

Perhaps this is an island, and leap is what I must do.

FEELINGS

Oh, the waves of feeling.

I know you'll pass very quickly.

As you're here,

allow me to

ENCAPSULATE and FRAME you.

UNFAMILIAR

(a monologue)

Monologue. Monologue. I'm speaking more and more in monologue. I have been, since the beginning of this funky old year. Monologuing my voice, my views, unfamiliar with the views of other people, monologuing my way through unprecedented ground, feeling my way around it, socially distancing from precious dialogue and my sacred mental wealth.

This is the space of the wobble. The discussions and debates, a thing of the past. Yeah well, I prefer dialogue, actually. Yeah. I mean… Does that? I mean, shall we? Shall we just have a dialogue instead?

Would that work for you? Because I would feel much less anxious.

SEE IT

I write, I write, I write
ALL the lines
filling up the page.

Answer me, answer me, answer me
I beg you.

I write, I write, I write
the answer comes through like
a flash of lightning:

REST.

She stops me in my tracks.

Rest. Then,
awaken.

HOW YOU CHANGE THE WORLD

Step off the merry go round.

Take a rest from it.

Slow down and see the scenery.

Breathe.

Reassess what is important and what is essential to you.

Buy a notebook and pen.

Start writing/drawing.

Dance.

Eat cake.

Sell your house and downsize.

Look at photos of yourself as a child.

See yourself with your innocence, your hopes, your wants, your wishes.

Feel them all. Cry them out. Write to your anger. Feel your pain. Laugh at how funny you were.

Marvel at how beautifully perfect you were.

How beautifully perfect you ARE.

It's NEVER TOO LATE TO LOVE YOURSELF,

to give yourself what your heart is craving for.

To live.

YOU ARE A VITAL and ESSENTIAL PIECE OF THIS JIGSAW.

We need you in all of your glory. The whole, integral you.

THE BIGGEST PIECE IN THIS?

Don't just talk the talk: WALK THE TALK.

Take action. Humanity is so worth it.

DO YOUR THANG

If you want to inspire, it is helpful for your head to be clear.

What practice clears your head?

What is your uniqueness?

What are you remarkable at?

Practice YOUR OWN way to be.

Do your thang. Whatever it is that comes straight from YOUR heart, not someone else's, just because it sounds good.

Drink your own elixir.

Do one authentically YOU thing today.

That's the first product that hits the shelf. That's what people feel. That's what inspires.

That's the money.

Stop wasting yourself being mediocre at lots of things; you shine at something.

Talk about it. Sing about it. Bake about it. Shine from your heart about it.

That is love.

That is compassion and all the feminine qualities that make a community thrive.

This is how we get unstuck from this stale, rigid, frigid world which you think is your reality.

Find your juices again and allow them to flow.

I AM WHO I AM

I always know who I am.

Even when I don't know who I am, at least I know

I don't know who I am.

SHOWER WISDOMS

If you operate out of your rational mind, you will not be open to the magic of change.

You're here because you are open to other realms; the possibility there is another way to live.

You understand what is past is passed and what is meant to crumble will tumble.

Are you meant to be at the frontline with your axe breaking down the walls?

Or are you in the inception phase of setting up the covenants of the new world?

We are the seeds for the foundations.

Break the connection.

YOU WILL KNOW MY VOICE

YOU WILL KNOW MY VOICE.

IT IS YOUR VOICE.

THIS IS '*THE*' VOICE.

SHE WILL KNOCK OVER YOUR HOUSE OF CARDS.

*YOUR TRUE ELEMENT **WILL** BE REVEALED.*

Part 3:

“Fear does not Heal”

FREEDOM OF EXPRESSION

Some days, '*Fuck You*' feels nice.

Though overall, '*Thank You*' feels better in the heart than a '*Fuck You*'.

The journey is long.

The journey is a constant teacher.

FREE FALL

(a monologue)

I'm free falling. I've been free falling for a few days. I've been free falling like: woah.

I see the body, I see the arms flailing about, I see the legs flailing and it's RAPID.

I try to hang on, hang on to the remnants of what kept me upright.

I hear the sound of traffic zooming by

I cling on

I cling on

I cling on

and my legs

keep going

keep going

keep going.

It's like I'm on a bike. I'm on a bike going downhill. Except, down this hill, there's a few stones and it's starting to go a little bit faster. I'm wearing a helmet, but it's shaking on top of my head. In fact, the helmet shaking on top of my head is making my head's insides rattle and all of a sudden, I am very conscious of the fact it's me, on a bicycle, I am not ONE with this bicycle and I am not ONE with the road and it is going way, way, WAY out of control and then…

The voice says: 'Slow down then.'

How do I slow down in this free fall?

How do I slow down in this free fall because, I don't actually know what I'm falling into?

A little bit like Alice in Wonderland, like falling down this rabbit hole and not knowing where the end is, not really knowing where I'm going, so that's why I'm going to try to CLING ON to every single last remnant of everything I have EVER known because, it's what's kept me alive, right? The busyness? The keeping going? The going back to that relationship, the going back to that job because the job gives me the money and the money gives me the house and the money gives me the car and gives me the clothes and gives me everything that helps me stay on a level except, what level is this? Because… I really am free falling.

STOP IT. STOP IT.

Right now, I am no longer free falling on this Earth, I'm on another planet.

It's something quite extraordinary. Feeling like the free fall into space where actually, il n'y pas de repères. Y a pas de repères. No markers as you knew them. As you recognise them. Those markers are now gone, those markers which you might have recognised.

The markers of Pub, Alcohol, Coffee, Shops. They've GONE. This is like a black hole. How long does this black hole go on for?

There comes a point I have to accept 'The Free Fall'.

Am I falling or floating?

This is me slowing down.

This is me slowing down, but I'm still in free fall.

I have moments of waking back up and trying to cling to whatever and I feel my body convulsing. I feel the convulsion. I feel myself trying to be sick and waking myself up out of this weird reality. But there's something bigger I can't fight against.

I can't fight against it. So, I free fall.

I free fall. There's nothing I can do about it. I observe the environment and everything around me has slowed - down.

There's a voice.

There's a voice, there's a very, very loud voice around me, like a layer of fear.

A layer of rules telling me what I should do, what I must do and I understand the need for that voice but here in this now moment, I don't need to hear that voice.

I KNOW I don't need that voice. It is not helpful.

I know this because as I look beyond the echo of the voice, I see the sun is shining; I can hear the birds.

I see there's healing.

I see the healing.

I see the healing.

Still, it slows down. Everything slows down.

I guess it comes to the point of, do I see there's nothing left for me to do but to allow for my body to softly land wherever it is going to land? Land. Or float. Or land.

Because now I'm so, so far away from what I thought were my umbilical cords and life forces that actually, I'm in a completely different space. Is this… Is this a cave? Is this space… A womb? What is this space?

I do know I'm safe.

SAFE. All that noise is still around me but I'm safe. I go back to my heartbeat. The one that's always been the same. The only way I can find myself. It's MY umbilical cord, my heartbeat. It's me.

Do I want IN? Or OUT? This is the edge.

STRONG. It's strong. While I lay here what happens? What can I feel? When I listen, to that heartbeat, it feels a bit like an injection of something doesn't it? Does it feel like paracetamol, like wine, like a drug? It's more.

It's divine power.

I'm in control in this place of 'not being in control' because the breath is me, I am the breath, I am this body, I am laying but WHO AM I?

There are people, beings, spirits, magical depths whispering to me. In this moment, I have no idea what day or month it is. I have zero idea where I am.

If I think about it too much, it sends me back into the whirlpool of free fall. It feels like a fine line indeed. The fine line of life and death.

I bring myself back out by slowly savouring those nourishing breaths. As I bring myself back out, I come round to the fact I can see, I can hear, I can touch, I can feel and I can taste. That must mean I am back in my physical body; therefore, I am ALIVE.

I am alive.

There's the question of why – is there also a question of how?

This space of holding, this space of laying down, of allowing the free fall and the surrender, could that be the medicine? Could that be what's worth investing in?

When you next come back to that state of surrender, could it be that because you are more accepting of it, more magic lands in your lap and in your heart?

How much is that worth? How much is life and vitality worth to you?

Is that worth less than your daily 365 large skinny caramel latte? Is that worth less than you buying more clothes to fill your wardrobe with? Less than your precious time running around everyone else? No judgement. Just questions.

That feeling of peace, having access to more of your stability and feel good so you can stand up on your own two feet and fly solo– is that not worth more than the RACE?

Think about what you are investing in this one life. You are the one investing in your running away from yourself, the fake umbilical cords. You are feeding somebody else's umbilical cord. Meanwhile, you deplete your life force more each time.

Invest in YOU. You.

That's the message of the Free Fall.

I COULD BE ANGRY

I could be angry at you because you don't notice,

I could be angry at you because you don't outwardly give me a sign you are interacting or involving yourself with what I am 'producing' for you,

I could be angry you seem to change the parameters of what is and what isn't acceptable,

I could be angry you're the one who chooses what is put forward - and what is not,

I could be angry you're the one who holds the key to the rule changes and I have no say in it,

I could be angry about all of those things

but REALLY, it's down to me.

It's down to ME to KNOW what I WANT TO SAY and WHY I want to SAY IT.

To say it in the way I want to say it.

Not because I'm trying to please you;

not because I'm bending to a whim that is not mine.

No.

THAT, you see, compromises MY integrity.

And MY integrity is the truth I stand in and the truth I stand for.

It's the absolute.

INTUITION DISSUASION

You are dissuaded from your intuition because

the dissuader is scared

of pain

of death

of losing their job.

They are scared of their own shadow.

LAID TO REST

Part 1: introduction

It occurs to me

perhaps the reason it's so hard to press pause and lay down,

is indeed because Rest IS the Ultimate Healer (you KNOW this from the depths of your bones).

To heal, one has to face;

To face can be confronting;

Confronting can upset so much.

Too much.

You see, I have been resting every day since I laid to rest in my breath as I bled out and crashed.

I returned with fire in my soul.

Resting away IS the message.

Slow down, SEE the scenery.

Not just what's around you. What's inside you too.

Therein lays the clincher as to your reluctance.

Part 3: "Fear does not Heal"

The scenery you have created feels too engrained, intertwined and complicated. To unravel this is just too much.

Part 2: fact

We live our lives overwhelmed. Everything a mountain.

When really, it is quite simple.

It's just one STOP at a time.

It is indeed up to you.

Your choice.

Your life.

YOU are responsible. Not the government or the doctors or the gatekeepers.

You have the power.

To find it, you Rest.

The Rest opens up ALL THE REST.

Part 3: can we handle the truth?

After the rest, what of that soul message I have been enjoying 'rendez-vous'ing with every day in my quiet depths like some illicit affair under the covers?

What about her? The one voice from the very beginning, the one who captivates the hope and feeling in people?

Can I take her hand, can we come through into the light together? Can I feel her, be her, wear her? In 'real' life, while I'm awake?

The actress

The writer

The storyteller

The fantasy woman my powerful creative mind is revealing?

Could it be that speaking out loud this simple truth of who I really am is as hard as YOU LAYING DOWN TO REST BECAUSE YOU KNOW THAT IT MEANS EVERYTHING TO YOU?

Then, it's just a matter of… what are you afraid of?

THE STORY OF THE DISCARDED FACE MASK

How fascinating and intriguing it is to me, when I go on walks and find hidden pieces of treasure the Earth has gifted me.

I come across objects from empty shells and sticks to bones, along with the occasional feather. I like to think about the story of the object and I'm quite happy to drift off into my thoughts, alone, should it even happen to concern a lone sandal, hanging from the branch of a tree, hoping to be reunited with its owner in a day or three.

Then, there are the horror stories. The ones like the dog walker who was kind enough to place their dog's poo in a bag and hang it up on a branch.

Or the pair of men's pants, shamed into flopping over a bush with no dignity, begging the question of "if the bush is wearing the pants, what is the human wearing?" (And… why?)

Every piece, with a story of its own. We can only guess or indulge ourselves into flights of fanciful imagination as to their adventures.

Then, there's this one.

For me, the saddest one of all. Perhaps the one which will shame the people of 2020.

Just like we are finding plastic wrappers from umpteen years ago, this will be the gravest indictment of all.

Not only were the people of this planet running with fear dripping through their pores, the fear contaminating and breeding more efficiently than any other breeding programme ever invented, they also decided to diarrhoea all over their keeper, maker and mother.

WOULD YOU HUG ME

(a monologue)

Part 1

If you saw me,

If you saw me in the street today, would you hug me?

If I asked you to give me a hug, would you hug me?

If I looked you in the eye, and asked you for a hug, would you say yes? Or no?

Would you feel better if the parameters were changed?

Would you look around and see if anybody is watching first?

Do you WANT to give me a hug?

Do you deeply desire to hug me but cannot bear the thought of getting into trouble for giving me a hug?

Is that the level of your hugging? Is that the depth of the contract of your hug?

Or is it deeper…

Part 3: "Fear does not Heal"

Do you love and feel for me, but do not want to come near because the fear of the responsibility of the possibility you may carry within you something so deadly you could transmit to me in the enveloping of your arms, would perpetuate this horror now not just within you, but to within me?

Does that belief extend to the 'fact' I also 'unknowingly and covertly' carry this horror within me which I would relay over to you and so on to all the people whom you then come into contact with? Is that what you believe?

It's been made so fogging complicated, hasn't it?

Let me break it down, human to human.

If I was dishevelled, if I was sad and lonely and heartbroken, and I needed a hug, would you give me a hug?

If, like a lost child, I didn't have the words to express all of the sadness, and the sadness was only apparent in my outwardly, messy appearance, the tired look in my eyes, if you could see my pain… but you also saw the barrier of your shame, would you still reach for the humanity inside you? Extend your arms and envelop them around me so that I might feel the sweet warmth of connection that you might feel and need too?

The making of magic from this basic spark of humanity, the magic spark of life itself?

Part 2

Where are you in this?

Are you deep in the midst of the complexities far removed from the possibility there is another way out?

Or, are you near to the circumference edge, where it's not a perfect outline, but there are little bumps in the circular wire fence, moulded shapes of the people who have banged themselves against it in order to break a little pocket of light and precious life-giving oxygen?

Do you know you are not alone?

Do you know there are so many who feel like you?

Do you know it's by opening up you meet with kindred spirit

and you

open yourself up to joy,

love,

connection

and

unity

and

community?

Part 3: "Fear does not Heal"

This is an unprecedented time.

Will you make decisions based on your primal human instinct or obey your masters?

TWIN MUSE

We speak so similarly; I get confused as to who had the original idea or notion. The jealousy rises.

She is brilliant (as am I).

She is popular (I don't feel it).

She is 'known' (I am not).

Feeling regression, not progression.

I love meeting with her. She fuels me (I fuel her).

I feel choked. She gifts me with the sweetest unexpected whole hearted gestures and accolades.

I can't fathom why I am such a shit friend, when all she does is remind me to keep returning to my solid core, remember who I am and what I'm doing it all for.

I don't know why I feel the need to separate us

when actually,

we are ONE.

We have been all along.

VOICE ON MUTE

I can't sing to the top of my voice because my voice is too loud.

Everyone will hear me.

That's why a stage
that's why a microphone
that's why the car
feels so good.

There's SPACE to be on purpose.
I want to sing.

I don't have a tiny voice.
It's almighty and powerful.

Part 4:

"We turn from the inside"

YOU HOLD YOUR LOCK AND YOU HOLD YOUR KEY

For the longest time, I have driven my second hand (and some) banger black Audi.

It coughs. It spurts. The windows moan as they crawl up and down.

Every day is now a gamble. The crash imminent and inevitable. It's just a matter of which corner.

On Sunday, the key remote gave up. Locked out and aghast, I took a breath and closed my eyes praying to the God who can see when lessons have been learned. I was ready for a sign.

I noticed a key slot concealed beneath the door handle.

How had I never spotted this before?

I slid the key into this long-forgotten lock.

The slightest of resistance gave way to the slickest of turns.

The car came to life in glistening white diamonds, a showcase version with all the upgraded options appearing right in front of my eyes. The seats, the steering wheel, the tyres, the roar of the engine, all dripping in its infinite conceptual design.

She had been there, hidden in plain sight, all along.

All I needed to do was breakdown and put the fricking key in.

REBIRTH

(as told by the angels)

How far, to which depths will you travel, to be reborn?

A slight change in your circumstances?

No. Maybe that won't be the trigger. It might help, as the change will alter the frequency of your energy indicating something noteworthy for you, but the doorway back to 'normal' may still hold you there. It's what you've known the longest.

'As sure as eggs is eggs', more will knock on your door, plugging away for your attention.

An illness. A death. A scare. A breakdown. An identity crisis. A near death experience. Your body and mind stretching to shapes it has never been before. A 'things are spiralling, I used to be able to control it and now it's gone to shit' type feeling. A change from all that was before.

The discomfort zone. A land with no safety markers. Uncharted territory.

Here, through the depths of the darkness is your guide. A hand or hands or voices, smiles, warmth, kind words, rest, soft whispers, strong vibrations, the sweet timely lyrics of a song. So many guides around you, talking with you the whole time, waiting for you to take the other door and leap into the new.

Just like birthing happens from inside the body, so does rebirth. From the rooted place of mystery and majesty it all came to be in the first place, where all is acknowledged and seen. Where all is made welcome. Welcome to feel all the rawness of laying it all to rest. Death. Roar it out, shout it out, scream it out, write it out, punch it out, cry it out.

The beauty of this arduous journey is you choose your position.

You are so worthy and capable.

We are with you the whole way until the end, whatever happens.

You are never alone.

SAFETY FIRST

I keep checking to see whether I've got my seatbelt on.
Then, I realise it's not a seatbelt I need;
it's knowing my integrity to my very core.

A BEAUTIFUL MESS

A *beautiful mess* is a space of growth. It encompasses the pre-requisite extremes.

'Beautiful' because if you can let go of the pressures, the comparisons and feel into what is YOU, whether that's dancing, art'ing' around, having a daily poo or not having 'the boss' on your back: you, my friend, have come home.

A *'mess'* because any semblance of what you thought you knew feels like a detached and distant memory. The disarray of not only feeling socially distanced from the things and the people, but your whole world imploding.

The beautiful mess of awakening to the fact in THIS house, you are THE ONLY ONE who can tidy up.

You can do this.

Pick yourself up off the floor.

Have a shower.

Put some perfume on.

Curl your eyelashes.

Get outside and listen.

Get inside and listen.

It's a beautiful mess.

THE CONTROVERSY OF BEING LIKED

(in the dark)

Being liked (in the dark) is like
being the lover in the affair.
They will never leave their wife.

No matter how good you feel
how good you look
how well you suck their cock.

You bring them all the excitement
of what an alternative life would be;
the spark of potential.

You give them LIFE.

In return,
they won't hold your hand in public.

They will cherish you, with ALL the gifts, ALL the fancy words, all the time IN SECRET.

They will never leave their wife.

The 'collective' story around that is

the woman never 'wins'.

She always stays in secret.

She is never going to be loved fully.

Is that why we have this primal instinct to admire from the darkness of our earphones and the time alone in the car?

Oh, there's another side to this story, if you will allow me to tell it.

She kept circling around the shit

she got fed up of the smell

she woke up

she dusted off her wings

and she fucked off.

ON PRIVILEGE, POWER & SERVICE

What is privilege?

A recognition? A gratitude? A right to something others don't and have to work EXTRA hard at?

When you don't have that privilege (you'll know what it is intuitively as you will have felt it), how does it feel? Where do you feel it?

Those privilege layers (skin colour, gender, religion, money, blah blah, brand of yoga leggings and all the other letters etc +) are 'just' that. Layers.

Wherever you are, whichever stage - there's a place right there in your body, YOUR BODY - that is YOUR PRIVILEGE and GODDESS GIVEN RIGHT: the freedom to breathe and feel into YOUR power.

You can have all the privilege in the world and never know what that power is.

That power - it keeps you alive.

That power - it gives you goosebumps.

That power - it connects you to the line of ancestors who lived for you to be here and connect to it so that you may ROAR with all your MIGHT, be everything you are and realise this truth:

it's not about having power, it's about service.

That privilege within will bring you everything you need. Go to it every day and soak up its wisdom. Follow it. That's the wisdom to follow. The one from inside your body.

TRANSPARENT

‘I feel transparent today’, I said.

I don’t really know what I meant.

I think I meant to say I felt a little bit see through.

Half, you can see me - half, you can’t.

I’m waiting for my bleed to arrive. She is in motion, waiting in the wings to come down for air. Until then, there’s a storm brewing within, in amongst this transparent state.

I do feel quite transparent indeed, like a jelly fish, like a ghost. Put your hand on me and it will go through. I don’t feel all there, but then, I’m not quite sure where I am either, which realm.

I don’t dislike feeling transparent; on the one hand, I feel absorbent, extra receptive to energies, extra sensitive to what is happening around me. I hear it and feel it all.

On the other, I also feel a little wide open. Kind of vulnerable. The arrow will go straight in. Then again, it will go straight back out and through. There’s a fluidity to transparency.

I wouldn't be satisfied with this for a whole 28 days. I prefer a little more firmness.

I don't feel as weak as a soapy bubble my kids would destroy in a nano second, neither do I feel angry. I feel… in between worlds.

Check-in.

My heart still beats. I know because I can feel it. My womb is moody, she's got some space she's stretching.

I don't mind that you can see through me.

Through my essence.

Just know, I'm seeing through you too.

TRUST THE NIGGLE

The niggle in me, every day, as I step outside the door is… I don't feel safe.

'Keep safe.' they say.

Well, I don't feel safe in a world of people wearing masks.

The whole of my being repulsed as I remember lives I didn't think I'd lived, when my eyes are forced to look at the tsunami of symbols of oppression which have scarred history, displaying my precious fellow humans as slaves.

Something visceral within my internal computer sounding 'Code Red!' as I approach masked humans in the street, in shops and school playgrounds. Every intelligent cell of my being knowing there is a malfunction.

My internal system, given to me from birth, enabling me to detect friend from foe, is being scrambled. We are not robots. I rely on being able to see and feel who you are.

This is not about me convincing you to change your mind.

You have all the capabilities inside you to make those decisions for you. You have everything at your fingertips. It's you who decides what you tune into.

I choose to tune into me and as I believe that me is made of the dust, the earth, the sky and this universe we are part of, I know I am right where I need to be.

If I am made of the elements all around me and I step outside the door listening, tuning in to their song, their message, then therefore, I am tuning in to myself. I know when the wind, the rain and the sunshine tell me it's time to take cover. I know when the warmth or the breeze is inviting me to dance with it. I see the life living. In the earth and in the sky. I am that life living. You are that life living.

I feel alive. I am VITAL. I also know I am mortal. I do not have the ultimate control yet I am free to choose. I am aware that in my cycles, within and outside my body, there is a full spectrum of opposites, part of our present every day. The light and the dark. The cold and the hot. The angry and the happy. We cannot avoid them. We are up and we are down.

Feel them. Feel them.

This is not me saying I do not care about you if I don't wear a mask. This is me understanding as humans, we have the right to trust our intuition, our internal signs communicating with us. We are not here to abandon ourselves. To listen and love ourselves is, to me, is how we care for one another.

Who are we to tell each other what we 'should' be doing?

How dare we think we are better than the next? That we know better than the next?

No one knows me better than I know myself. I am my best ever and most exciting roller coaster relationship I've ever had. My intuition is not against me. I have done so much work to get here and still have a long road of adventures ahead. My intuition is made from the earth and the stars and the dust. It is ME. In the same way that your intuition is YOU.

The equation is so simple: if I don't stand up for ME, I don't stand up for my children and I don't stand up for you.

This is not about division. I'm not here to fight. I get angry. I roar. Loudly.

I'm here to feel deeply within and act on it.

My soul has so much depth, it has the capacity to make you weep as you recognise in there a vibration from when you were deep in your mother's womb. Way before that, in fact. Way before, when you were stardust and part of the sound of creation herself.

The soul. The sound that gets you in the back of the neck. Those goosebumps that dance around your lower back and thighs when the whole of your being is locked into an inexplicable, indescribable moment of ecstasy.

This is about personal responsibility.

If you agree with something, know why you do. That's your integrity.

If you abide by a rule, abide with integrity and abide by it with all it is asking of you and not half of the rules.

I don't need you to wear your mask to look after me. I'm looking after myself.

I need you to look after YOURSELF, first and foremost. You are free to choose to wear your mask if you feel safer for all the reasons you have told yourself, but don't EXPECT others to do it for you.

YOU LOOK AFTER YOU.

This means looking into all the ways which make you FEEL SAFE AND AMAZING AND STRONG IN BODY, MIND AND SOUL. Now tell me honestly: do you feel the messages being pumped out are giving you this?

My niggle is I don't see a world of people expanding their minds, bodies and soul.

I see a world of people IN FEAR. I see retraction.

That's not how I breathe. That's not how I am meant to live on this planet in this lifetime.

It's scary being seen naked, but we're all the same underneath. I have nothing to hide or run away from.

I choose to trust myself because how we are made is so exquisitely intelligent, it has the power to unlock humanity like we have never experienced.

TREE WISDOM SPOOKS

In conversation with a magnificent Scots Pine tree in Portal Woods, it's wisdom spooks spoke of cracks.

They oozed from its trunk. Green moss, zig zagged and vertical, with golden thread allowing breath to come through.

Leaning in, I made out a soft whisper:

'Expose the tracks, expose the cracks.'

What if I shone light on the cracks? What is underneath? Who is to be exposed and rebirthed from those confines? In that moment, I hear the breaths, the rumble in the ranks.

The spooks continued:

'Humanity is locked up inside. Take them out. Blind the cracks with light, inject light. Stealth, soft and invisible. Watch the light peel the walls wide open. Rejoice at the sight of them running out, naked and free.

You are poised, prepared to hold the ones who want to play and polish their gold to rebuild heart led structures.

The head led structures are crumbling.

Go where there is space and plant your heart led seeds there.'

Part 5:

"I haven't lost my mind. I've gained my soul"

I HAVE A DREAM

Document the story

Play

See the story

Be you

Tell the story

All the way.

HAIL THE WISDOM OF POO

Every day, I write.

It may be shit, but it cleanses.

As I write out the deep stuff,

sometimes I physically need to poo.

What an ultimate sign from my body.

I hereby very solemnly and proudly declare myself the embodiment of detoxification, letting go and cleansing.

WOW.

Hail the wisdom of poo

(who knew all those years my IBS was a load of shit too).

I am amazing.

I WELCOME

I welcome all I have and all I am

(light and dark)

I welcome my radiance, my soul, my KNOWING

(along with anger, provocation and meanness)

I welcome joy, writing, speaking; the goosebumps of soul connection

(along with bad hair days, ugly bras and 'bonkers' thoughts)

I welcome glow, smiles; the freedom to be ME

(along with THAT voice)

I welcome THAT voice of shadows. I love to explore its source.

(Sometimes I voice on paper. I love how aware and conscious I am of the contrast of my light and my dark)

I welcome the contrast, the stretchy place of extremes while I sit in the middle, the edges clearing. I see how when they meet, their energy comes from the same source; the deducing of this being a matter of perspective, discernment, inner work and a soupçon of investigative flair.

I focus on the feeling this welcoming brings and slowly, it pieces together. Right there in the midst of the dark.

THAT voice brings me sight.

I ask for its teaching.

It tells me all I have, all the gifts, they are the blending of fire and air; stirring passion for life, firing inspiration.

I'm here to make you feel. It's all divinely timed.

You're welcome.

BONKERS

(a monologue)

Let’s talk about ‘Bonkers’.

Let’s FLIP REVERSE IT.

What if ‘bonkers’ was the new normal? What if ‘bonkers’ was the actual normal?

What if we’ve actually been conditioned against ‘*bonkers*’?

You see, it’s ‘bonkers’ to change your mind about something every two seconds.

It’s ‘bonkers’ to leave a relationship even when you know it’s done because you know? It’s *bonkers*.

It’s ‘bonkers’ to leave a really ‘good’ job when you’ve got a really good pension at the end and all you’ve got to do and stay for another 10, 20 years… It’s *bonkers*.

WE STAY COMMITTED.

We stay committed to the cause.

What? What’s that?

What do you mean, REST???

It's 'bonkers' to rest. There's so much to do! So much WE HAVE to DO!!

It's 'bonkers' to be selfish.

It's 'bonkers' to follow your heart.

Darling, all that stuff, 'following your heart', listen, that's what happens to the lucky people.

That's the stuff that happens in films, on the telly. The stuff of fiction.

No, no, no, no. No. You are *BONKERS.*

Life's HARD, alright? It's hard.

LET'S FLIP REVERSE IT.

Bonkers. Bonkers. Coercive abuse is bonkers.

Bonkers is being exhausted physically, mentally and emotionally for your whole entire life.

Bonkers is being caught up in the wheels of a 'made up' RUSH.

You see, WE COMMIT. We WORK TOGETHER. We CONTRIBUTE to the economy and society.

AT ANY GIVEN COST.

The cost of mental health.

The cost of devaluing the human.

Bonkers is when we ACTUALLY believe that WE ARE WORTHLESS,

that everything in our lives is too much and we are less than.

Bonkers is when you do not teach the VALUE in the things that don't 'BRING IN THE MONEY'.

Because it's 'bonkers' to speak for yourself.

It's 'bonkers' to think for yourself.

It's 'bonkers' to TRUST YOURSELF. Isn't it?

Here are a couple of my personal reviews as I've gone on my 'bonkers' journey:

"*She's gone bloody mad!*"

"*At first, I thought you were BONKERS and then it all started to make sense. The words, the movement.*"

What if taking a pill for the vast majority of your bleeding life is the bonkers thing to do?

What if NOT BEING IN YOUR TRUTH was just the ultimate fudging up of your own humanity?

What if we flipped the script, we got to KNOW our ultimate TRUTH inside of our unique selves?

What 'bonkers' would reveal from there?

MY PRAYER

I write hoping for poetry,

some words to make me 'famous'.

I write to invoke the universe and invite her to journey through.

I write on my phone though it's time for my bed.

I write, begging for insight and inspiration.

I write though I know, it won't come right now. It won't come at all. I'm too fussed, too bothered, too frustrated by it all.

I want to feel the goosebumps and the soul of everything;

I want to feel connected to all the passion, the artists, the brave ones who dare to bare.

'Pipe dreams, pipe dreams - you're too old (perhaps your children will play these roles).'

But singing... but acting... but oh, my soul.

To stand, recite and let out pure gold.

Go back to basics, back to the start. But which start? The start when I dreamed of being on stage? Doesn't everyone have that dream at one stage?

Is this tiredness...? Dear soul, give me a script, some words and I'll connect straight away.

Give me a tune, a poem, I'll translate it into soul dust. I'll make you feel, I'll make you goosebumps, I'll make you remember everything. I'll bring on those tears of joy, of sadness, of feeling something deep. I'll make you feel 'cos feeling is the way; for if we don't feel: we are dead.

Before I step on, I wonder how I'll do it. Then I take a breath. I am prepared. I wanted to do this. I've been training for lifetimes. I know it. I have rehearsed it time and time again. I hear my voice, I feel the words, I see myself as I act it out.

I step in, I am on. I am transcended.

This stuff right here is the real deal. I know it. This is the stuff I wouldn't want to read out to anyone because this... comes from me. The hardest to confess to because, it's the dream. The everything. To earn a living by sharing, conveying soul.

Who am I to think this may be?

So, I play with my soul and twinkle it with a passion for women's secrets, how to love, breathe, give birth and be reborn. For empowerment, for living one's best life and for the service of greater things.

(*and so it is.*)

HOW SHE CAME

She came about daily, discreetly, creeping softly, within my highs and lows.

She knew I was the one.

The one who could embody her.

She knows it’s my life’s work.

That’s why she’s chosen me.

I’m strong enough to go there and soft enough to share.

THE LONELY KID IN THE PLAYGROUND

A house. The open kitchen/diner.

A washing machine is on in the background.

***Sophie** is a bright, confident, French/British trail blazer on a career break from 15yrs as a detective in a police family. After several 'career' changes, she is giving herself the lead part in her life. It is simultaneously exhilarating and exhausting.*

She is sat at the table, shoulders slumped.

***Mark**, wise beyond his years, is the long suffering 'other 'alf'. He is pulping tomatoes.*

SOPHIE *(sighs)* I feel like the lonely kid in the playground.

MARK Isn't it your own playground though?

SOPHIE *(sad face)* Yes - but I'm playing by myself.

MARK *(ceases 'pulping of tomatoes' action)* You know, the truly happy children who play by themselves in the playground will be joined by other children who want to play with them, because the happy lonely child is having all the fun.

(They look at each other awkwardly, as if weighing up the wisdom of those words, unsure of what to say until Sophie startles into life and notes down those exact words.)

End of scene.

#NOTSORRYCLUB

All these fucking '*not sorry*' and '*I am an unapologetic woman*' clubs,

here's a #notsorry truth for 2021 no one is willing to swallow:

it's ok to be a rebel about ANY OTHER FUCKING THING right now than the ACTUAL FUCKING ISSUE OF:

WE ARE BEING FUCKED.

THE GOLD RUSH CHALLENGE

The gold is coming. Like a slow purification, clarification process. It is coming.

It's already here, actually. It's building. It feels huge. Amazing. Powerful. Abundant. Total gold.

Imagine you are a gold searcher, like back in the day of the gold 'rush'. There you are, for the umpteenth time, in the stream of water, with your pasta strainer, hovering over. There's sand. Mud. Algae. Bugs. A snail. A shell. An old piece of plastic. A face mask. All coming at you, thick, fast and 'gungey' at 100mph (it's not called a rush for nothin').

This is the process of clarifying, slowing down and sifting for the gold.

Then, a nugget. A piece of gold.

You have come to the end of Challenge 1. You practiced patience.

The process has taught you if it matters to you this much to get the gold, you will show up, through the sand, the mud, the 'everything-but-the-gold'.

It may even be you saw wisdom (*as gold*), sifting through the murk.

You now have a gold nugget in your possession.

You want more.

You invent Challenge 2.

Allow me to ask – what did you want the nugget for in the first place? Have your motivations changed since you began? Has the process allowed you to appreciate its value?

What then, then? Do you reassess what you have? Do you already have gold in reserves within your streams of mud, snails and algae only recently found on this journey? Those which you would not have named '*gold*' at the start?

What do you want with the 'Gold', gold searcher?

How much do you need? Where will it be redistributed?

Once you find it, can you take what you need? Leave some for the others to go on their journeys and not deplete the source's resources?

Once the real value of YOUR gold has landed with you, how satisfied and full do you feel?

What would be a like for like exchange, how will you align the frequencies of that energy so the gold ripple keeps on and on?

THE TRUNK OF LIFE

The fallen twisted wobbly trunk laid bare
waiting
being
laying
witnessing.

I made the choice to play
up and down it
fell off, got back on
bounced on it
slowed down
went faster; stopped.

Found my balance
breathed and knew
I'd just played at the game of life.

THE MISSING PIECE OF THE JIGSAW

Has anyone seen my missing piece?

What even is my missing piece?

I've looked everywhere.

(ASK)

'I've come for your help. I hear you see things. I want to know what I need to do so I can go straight to it. It's so close. So close.'

'*Yes, I'll help you. Why don't YOU suggest as to where YOU feel it may be?*'

(QUESTIONS)

Is it Lost? *No*

Chewed by the dog? *No*

Caught up in the mix of another person's jigsaw puzzle? *No*

Will I ever find it? *Yes.*

'Give me a clue…'

'This piece is the hardest to find (it is camouflaged).'

'Why???'

'It camouflages when you look too hard for it. Your forceful attentions repel it. It longs to dance the rumba of being uncovered, re-discovered, remembered.'

(TRUST)

'Relax. Let go. Close your eyes from the world of SEEING. Come within. Breathe. Slow down.'

There it is. There it was.

In the palm of my hand all along, coded within the ley lines of the ancient stories of the ancestors, guiding me all along.

PETA PAN

I saw a girl with a pink scarf and a purple jacket balancing on a fallen birch trunk.

She was alone.

No dog. No family.

I thought she was a girl because she was smiling and playful.

As I got closer, I saw she was a woman. A grown up. She looked up and saw me waiting for my turn. I didn't want her to hurry, I could see she was having fun. She had found my play place in the middle of the forest and I didn't mind sharing.

I enjoyed watching her so much, I said: 'you can come to my playground again tomorrow if you like!'

She smiled back and said she would most definitely be back.

GRAVE DIGGER FINDS GOLD

A man was digging in the dark
like a grave digger, unlawful.
I caught him right there, behind my gate.
I stood above him, looking down

'What on earth are you doing?'
'Miss, I've found gold and treasure. It's all down below!'
'Show me!' I said.

With a flick of his spade, he produced
eleven pink plastic pens
and a 2001 lined diary.

MY PONTOON BY THE RIVER

(part 1)

A RIFF ON WHAT I DO BEST

Swans glide, fish paparazzi sparkle at me.

When you're a bird and you fly, dreams must seem so much closer. Taking the view from the sky, the little things seem nit-picky and insignificant.

When you fly, you can see the world you love. It's within your sights.

You can see it, so you can go there. It's easy.

I am a writer. A dreamer. My favourite recurring dream is the one where I can fly. I float, I fly. FREE.

I'm here today because I feel asphyxiated. I'm in the autumn of my cycle but it feels wintery and bleak. INSIDE.

Here I am, OUTSIDE, by the river Deben. On 'my' pontoon, a place I have returned to alone countless times and with friends and family on rare occasions.

It's summer. I love the sounds as the ever-moving water streams through the gullets. I love the croaks, the tweets and the chitter chatter of the river traffic. The vast expanse of the ever-changing sky; sunny one minute, cloudy the next.

I love the houseboats. I imagine. I wonder who lives there and why. To live on a house boat must be a deliberate choice?

Do these people work? What do they do? Do they own? Do they rent? What of their view?

Are they happy?

Are they artists? Writers? Painters? Dreamers? Weirdo nature lovers? PIRATES?

They have access to a piece of dry land over the walkway. PRIVATE, it says. UNAUTHORISED ACCESS. What's in this wonderland? A washing line? A vegetable patch? The secret to life?

Then over the way, beyond 'our' side (the side of 'my' pontoon, moored houseboats and walkers enjoying a stroll along the windy path), beyond the water and the muddy landscape, greenery and wild grasses adorn the opposite shore. The land strangely hilly for Suffolk, mini forests of tall trees contour the horizon, the colour green peacocking.

There are boats moored out. Small boats, newer boats, moored. Floating. Waiting for a ride.

Then, there are the older ones. Weathered. In bits. Still standing, stuck in the mud and preserved, allowing the elements to welcome them back to their original state; serving as gateways of memories to the eagle-eyed wanderer.

The Anglo Saxons came up here. The Anglo Saxons chose this land over the shore, at Sutton Hoo.

A couple of sumptuous looking properties over there, on the dry land with their own mooring and outhouses.

Who lives there? What do they do? Are they happy?

Do they own the land? The house? How have they come to be here? Do they appreciate it?

Are they art gallery owners from London? Ancestors of the 'Lords of the Land'? Lawyers, famous writers secluding themselves to access the land of their imagination? Or is something more sinister lurking there?

The wind is rising. Now and again, I get the delicious whiff of the incense stick I am burning, at home in this space. I feel so present here. Blessed.

This is 'my' pontoon. My temporary view. I do not own it, as in 'on paper', yet, every time I come here, it stands empty, waiting for me to take a ride.

So, I go for the ride.

Every time, I take the time. I open up, I feel. I listen.

It feels good to fly from here.

MY PONTOON BY THE RIVER

(part 2)

A RIFF ON THE INDULGENCE OF SPACE

Feeling hemmed in and needing space, a memory of old came to mind of a conversation with my harassed Detective Inspector. She was the first female head of Special Branch, spinning a vast assortment of plates in high heels and suits.

I shared with her this bonkers idea that I would love to see available the gift of offering women the opportunity to book an empty space, just for themselves. There was no clear picture in my mind, though it wasn't a hotel to rent by the hour. More like a room, a place, a space, where you were not reachable, for however long you desired.

What strikes me is that this was eight years ago. Way before kids. I had ALL THE SPACE I DESIRED at that time: single, own car, own flat; whatevs: #independentwoman

I didn't appreciate it. Yet, the oxygen of space was the dream all along before I even knew what it was like to not have it.

Is it right what you dream for others is what you dream for yourself?

I know this sentence is a regular in my life: 'I NEED SPACE!'

What is this? What does it mean? What will I do with this SPAAACE? I have at times felt a pang of fear about this NEED of mine for empty SPACE. Do I not love my partner and kids? Does it take me back to all the moments my mother, grandmother and every other mother through time must have CRAVED for space on so many levels and not had it?

Space is not a time to THINK. It's a time to be. It's pointless applying rationale or logic in that precious space. The space is the space of opening your heart and seeing all the universe is gifting right in front of your eyes, right there in that spacious, precious moment.

SPACE IS OXYGEN and you create all the 'things' from there.

Here's another nugget: it's not about everyone else moving Heaven and Earth for you to have it but for YOU TO CHOOSE YOURSELF, INDULGENTLY TAKE IT AND BREATHE IT ALL IN.

There's your medicine.

MY PONTOON BY THE RIVER

(part 3)

A RIFF ON BRINGING IT HOME

Welcome to my dream life, a simultaneous marvel of sometime in the near future and right here in this very moment.

Before the house by the river and the floaty kimonos, the book deals and stories made into films, I would sit on my rickety pontoon, in the fresh air, by the river Deben. I would bask in this energy where nothing is forced and everything just flows. I realise now, I was rich and abundant all along. I felt it back then. I feel it right now.

What I do these days is not much different; I still write by the river, by the water. I still dream worlds into being.

I have laughter in my life. My writing, my voice, my talks, my shows, they hold people in a space of voyage within.

I have the courage to follow my heart, my gut, my soul. I know that living in my flow inspires others to tap into their own inner treasures also.

I dance through lines with ease and grace.
I know emotion and the fullness of its palette. The spectrum is vivid.

I have a collection of stories which soothe, confront and enliven.

Actors read my monologues.

The walkers who would walk along the swirly path behind me, as I sat in my earlier life pontoon, they would wonder: who is she? What is she writing? Is she famous?

Maybe the pontoon has a plaque with my name on it.

Maybe I'm writing this from the grand house opposite this pontoon on the riverbank.

(FLIP REVERSE IT. What's on the other side of you?)

MY PONTOON BY THE RIVER

(part 4)

A RIFF ON SIGN LANGUAGE

Time to leave, pack up and set off for home.

As I walked away, as I said goodbye, I saw the man who looks like my father.

For the third time now, he has come into my path.

He lives on a houseboat.

Today, he was in the boat yard tinkering on repairs.

What's this about?

Is this the life my dad wanted to live?

Is this the life I want to live?

Is this a sign showing me a parallel life, an alternative scenario? A deleted scene from the part where we decided to follow our hearts?

A 'there is never just one reality available to you' wink?

I love these signs.

Part 5: "I haven't lost my mind. I've gained my soul"

I leave the pontoon with a river of writing today.

A river of flow (literally- I am *desperate* for a wee).

YOU ARE WHAT YOU LOVE AND NOT WHAT LOVES YOU

A thought, a moment, about the people in my life, all the women; friends, best friends, new acquaintances, soul sisters, family, awake or not, on your journey, at whichever stage you are, courageous as anything, doing the best you can and showing up every single day.

To all of you, I thank you for inspiring me

I am grateful for having met you.

In this moment, I am full of love and gratitude.

We are witnessing a rising of humans as bright stars, shining beacons, lighting up one by one from the foggy runway, clear in their mission to heal and resolve shit in the world.

I am steady in my resolve to serve with all my heart.

I'm embracing love right now. Because I am what I love.

Part 6:

"I'm not scared, I'm sacred"

CALLING

I write and I read it out.

That's the bread and butter.

The inner voice to the outer voice.

Source to source.

FOR YOU

I'm writing to you, finder of stones

& feathers

& bones;

awe and fascination gatekeeper of the indescribable magic of nature.

You, who knows you are a mere grain of sand in the scheme of the universe, yet simultaneously, are EVERYTHING and ENOUGH.

You, who knows you are an untapped resource of all sorts of uniqueness and powerful gifts to lift up another human being, which in turn will change the course of this world.

I'm speaking to you, who knows the old structures are no longer fit for purpose.

You, who knows that this is the long game, that you may not see the full manifestation of the work you put in today as this is for your descendants' eyes.

You, who wants to change YOUR world NOW, because to not see the direct result is fine and to know that every moment of presence in the now is the key to unlocking your process. This is manifestation itself.

You know to free yourself is to free another.

You know doing the inner work isn't easy. You know through your intuition and discernment. You choose people who are an enthralling match for you, to bounce vibes off and to hold while we wonder, cry and exhale it out.

You know you are being contacted by other beings, whether they be spirits passed on, or other energies from other dimensions.

You haven't got all the answers and this thrills you, because you LOVE to learn.

You have come this far on your survival instincts and your wit.

Now, you are being called to go deeper. You know there's a divine purpose with your name on it.

You love humanity. You've made mistakes. You've felt ashamed. You have begun to delve into this, either by writing or speaking to it whilst out in nature. You have begun the process of forgiving yourself.

You understand inside of you is the child full of fire and glory who never went away. When you close your eyes and connect to your heart centre, you meet her there, in proud awe of her superpower and the recognition of that cheeky little smile.

She is you and you are her.

You are the solid sacred Mother Earth and always have been.

We need you. Are you ready?

SELF-ACTUALISATION

What will they think?

What will they say?

Will they even notice?

What's the worst that can happen?

What's the best that can happen?

So what if I don't know the next step?

So what if I am shaking?

So what if I haven't worked out a strategy?

So what if I don't have a website,

a HOOK 'em in ONE LINER,

a menu of services?

SEE,

I use magic.

It lands in my lap.

I land in yours.

Together, we make magic and we feel alive.

Like the BUZZiest pill you've ever taken, pepped up for it.

For I am PEACE and I am LIFE and I know how to activate my voice in order to activate yours.

Prepare for self-actualisation.

I have it all written already.

POST NATAL ORGASMIC REFLECTIONS

Laying in my warm bed, I'm alone. I know it's been a while. Since I felt down there, since I looked. From this place, I birthed my baby. I have not been ready. But now I'm alone. I'm warm. I ponder. I wonder. The Breath. The deep connection. The moment of perfect fusion, the deep connection. The orgasm. Natural Pain Relief. My recovery in my post-natal state. My pelvic floor.

My mind takes over. What am I left with? Is there any pleasure left? This place of shakti, of power, this sacred space, my womb, my vagina, my root. I'm healing from the inside out. I simply have to let go. Take deep breaths and allow myself to feel, to re-connect. With that space. The place of empowerment not embarrassment.

It strikes me as I feel my way to my yoni that after birthing, it's amazing to feel pleasure from there again. This right here, it's not about sex, it's about nurture. This right here, is self-care.

As I let go, I peel away the post birth layers. The purity of being 'in the moment'; no need to be groomed or showered.

This is my intimacy. Allowing myself to luxuriate and be fully attentive to the sensations. Allowing myself to heal some wounds. I consciously loosen my jaw, free up some stagnant energy.

The wounds are in my head. They have been all along. I start to radiate from within. I feel it come. I feel like a Goddess. This truly feels like Heaven on Earth.

This is the ultimate secret to love and connection: re-know yourself alone. In the sanctity of you alone.

Re-learn yourself. Be patient with yourself. Pleasure, not pressure. Your partner can wait.

Your body. YOUR body. No one else's.

Honour yourself and treat yourself with sacred care.

I BELIEVE IN MAGIC

If magic is just an illusion and doesn't fit in with serious adult life, then why does the church speak of miracles?

Magic is whatever you want it to be. I believed in magic powers my whole childhood; I just didn't know what form they took.

I joined the police and was 'sworn in'. I received my 'powers' to search and to arrest.

I lived my life in the power of my independence after a marriage break up. My magic being my inner strength carrying me through all along.

Then the power of birthing. Lactating. Bleeding. Dying. Crying. Laughing. Feeling. Connecting. Soul levelling. RESTING. The magic of being alive on this Earth, at this time. The magic of being so rested that you can connect to your soul and let her speak through words, vibration, dance, chopping carrots, painting nails, WHATEVER IT MAY BE THAT IS YOU, DEEP INSIDE, BRINGING YOU JOY... there's your magic power.

Go, meet the feeling. It has no age boundary, no ceiling.

Go experience why the hell it means so much to you.

THE ANGEL SAID TO REST

Do you know how much you light up when you close your eyes?

Do you know how much you glow?

Do you know how the contrast of your deepest dark and your lightest light merges into one while you take rest?

HEART SPACE

My heart space is my magic space.

From there, I love my children and all my loves.

From there, I love myself.

From there, I love myself.

Except. Except.

Where is the love today?

The key is in my heart space, the space is in the heart space.

So,

where is the love today?

It went away with lack of sleep.

It went away with firing on the pressure.

It went away when I forgot myself.

My heart space needs me. I need my heart space.

So, for five minutes, I will stand or sit up tall, open my arms wide and take some deep breaths. I will feel the air come in and spread from the centre of my heart all the way to the end of my fingertips.

I will be this open today, on repeat, to flood the love back in.

This is my step one.

My heart space.

WAKE UP TO YOUR INTUITION

Your intuition is guiding you to be reading these words, to listen to this voice. Feel, right here, there is a reason you are being called.

There is nothing better in this world than the feeling of warmth, authentic connection, welcome and nurturing acceptance. In a world where most of time, we do not feel welcome, know this:

You are precious. You matter. You are powerful beyond your wildest thoughts.

You have your own potent medicine cupboard overflowing within you.

You live in a world which makes you feel unsure and stupid most days.

A world where the others are right, you are to follow, you are to disregard your own intuition and body wisdom.

Wake up.

Wake up.

Wake up.

You were created by magic.

You are magic.

Magic has only bountiful treasure in store for you.

YOUR DESTINATION IS HERE

There is supposed to be silence.

Silence of the voice. The external voice you can hear and sounds all sorts of sweet, melodious, sore and angry. My external voice is silent.

In this quiet, what of the voices inside? When you listen, there are quite a few.

This morning, the ones in my head order me to be quick, have a shower, grab my notebook and write in time, in time for having breakfast and then in time for expressing my milk (which I am finding difficult).

As I write this, I feel like it's TOO MUCH, so, I say to these voices: 'Oy you! Shush. Slow down.'

I hear another one I recognise. It's her:

'YOUR DESTINATION IS HERE. Your destination is here. What delights can you see, feel and hear, right now?'

There she is. The 'she brings it all together' voice. The clarity.

She's not anything in particular and she is everything at the same time.

This voice, right now, is writing these words. She directs me to open my eyes.

This moment. This destination. It's all meant.

This moment to absorb. To be.

I needed this space. I needed this time to meet her again. I'm grateful she is within me.

She flows; an unstoppable creation of nature. In this now moment, we merge.

My destination is here for all the stories to come
My destination is here for all the joy they bring
My destination is here for this wonderful sweet kick ass voice of the universe
to remind me I am home in the vessel of my flesh and bones.

In the silence, you'll hear, your destination is here.

TIDAL TEACHINGS

The river had her skirt pulled up, exposing Mother Earth's otherwise covered sacred lands. As she caught me peeking into her peaks, truths, varicose veins and stretch marks, she said:

'Come on, *really* look, I'm not afraid. Everything you see here is reflected in all of you.

You may see mud, trenches, places vulnerable and open to the elements; you may also see a land of opportunity, feeding the wildlife, showing you a treasure map all the way to your roots; these stories beneath that stay in your subconscious and resurface with each cycle.

One day, you will be ready to explore the fullness of this journey of extremes, you will feel the flow of the tide in and the tide out.

You will know the time for delving into the creases and dark corners will be followed by still waters, held, until the next time, when you allow yourself to return and maybe this time, at the end of the crease, you find the gold.'

This time is now. The gold is abundant.

CHOICE

I don't want to get in the queue

because to queue

is to ask to be chosen

by people who decide.

I DECIDE.

I HAVE ALREADY CHOSEN MYSELF.

WOMAN

We need to rebuild and reclaim.

Stop and consider this current of gender neutralising and political correctness.

As of 2021, it is the WOMAN, whether you spell it with an ‘x’, a ‘b’ in the middle or use a symbol, who provides the container for the backbone to build itself along with the eyelashes and the heart.

The life inside has its own path. Its own way.

The woman alone hosts this fragility. This strength.

This miracle.

This is what is being lost.

This is what is at risk (when we all strive for EQUALITY).

ON PLAIN PORRIDGE AND BEING HUMAN

Upon reflection on all the ingredients which make up the social media algorithmic sauce that gives us MORE reach, more likes, more, more, MORE, I was reminded of a friend of mine who would always say: 'why mess with perfection?'

She was the one who liked a jacket potato with a simple knob of butter, a crumpet in all its toasted glory; porridge without fancy accoutrements.

She liked to go back to nature and allow it all to be.

We forget that at our essence, inside, there is nothing to add.

It is all there already.

The love, the graft, the raw deal, the flow.

The grace, the work, the lessons.

The most important essence of that is being human. It absolutely is the starting point. This is what WE ALL SHARE.

BEING HUMAN. Relating, sharing, loving, messing up, exchanging, giving, taking, empowering, awakening, hearing, FEELING from our hearts.

All those things, first and foremost, before the external add-ons that we inevitably develop attachments towards.

Simple, raw and real.

Ever wonder why it is that difficult to be on the same page?

Why we see so much hate and division? Why we are run by systems of fear?

I suspect it's all exposing itself for a reason. Like a scared angry beast who has been messed around with too much, for too long. Over exposed, undervalued and starved of the knowing at the heart of the beast, is HUMANITY, unravelling to bring itself back into the human consciousness and evolve.

The key, not in destruction and ignorance but in the radical responsibility of self for the purpose of the collective.

The plain'ness' and splendour of one single human and all their naked promise. Why mess with this?

THANK YOU

I see you on your way,

returning to the Earth.

You are a thing of beauty,

exquisite, finely layered and interwoven;

peeling back, giving back.

Thank you for your service.

For being here every day, doing that thing you do

I see you.

We are not the few, but the many.

We are the backbone.

A closing thought.

The story is never finished.

It lasts for eternity.

It ripples and dances through tidal cycles of time

never ending, always evolving.

Sisters are in sacred communion, casting spells on
invisible ink in nature portals.

Art, ritual and magic are the norm nourishing

our new world.

Merci infiniment.

À très bientôt.

PS: the next one is about spies.

ACKNOWLEDGEMENTS

The surreal moment when you find yourself at the keyboard typing the 'Acknowledgements' section of your first book…

The surreal moment you realise that you've written a book – and it is going to be published.

Writing an intimate book is no mean feat. I've been writing this for years. It's taken so many different forms. This is inner work on a canvas sewn with golden magic dust from my unfiltered heart. A lot was cleansed and cleared through this process.

I knew I'd write at least one book in my life, and here's the first. Going through the roller coaster of telling people what you're up to, seeing question marks over faces when they don't quite get the vision and keeping going anyway. So many moments arise when you're so deep into what you're putting together, it doesn't make sense anymore and you tell yourself it's a load of rubbish, no one will want to read it, it's self-indulgent. Then you get a beep on your phone with a heart-warming coded message, a quote, a poem, or you step outside the door to be held by nature and you know to keep going.

A massive process in this has been to surrender into trust and be open to receive the love of the people around me as fuel.

I am so grateful for the rocks in my life.

First and foremost, I acknowledge my spirit, for knowing there were stories to be shared, to keep living in play and documenting it. To the ‘me’ as baby, little girl, adolescent, adult and ever-expanding curious self, for not abandoning myself and for believing. Totally #notsorry (wink) for putting myself at the top of this list.

I’m eternally grateful to Mark, my love, my heart, for having the upmost faith in me, for being a boulder, a tower of strength and the kind of human being who knows intuitively that space is crucial. I love you. I thank Mark’s mum’s spirit Brenda, for guiding him this way.

To my children Leo and Eleanor – it’s all for you and your children and their children. Keep shining, beautiful free people.

To my parents Denise and Antoine, who provided me with reams of experiences to regale over during the course of my ‘inner work research’. For not getting in the way of my many life decisions and quietly cheering me on from France.

To my brother Julien and sister Johanna, who share the letter ‘J’ without me, in whose smiles and laughs I instantly feel connected to bloodlines; you are part of me every step of the way.

To my grandmothers, grandfathers and all the ancestors in spirit, guiding me all along, I feel you in my life, I hear your messages. I am your voice. I love you.

Thank you to the artist known as SOPHIE for the exquisite art adorning the cover, for the countless hours together soul consulting, heart holding and nature bathing. For being the clap over the process line and the second moon. It's an absolute honour playing at life alongside you.

To Jo, my best friend, thank you for seeing me in all my various shapes and guises throughout the years, for loving me, for wanting to understand, for believing in the good in people; I could go on for years. For being 'Auntie Jojo', swimming instructor and ultimate snack provider to my kids, thank you infinitely.

To Uma Dinsmore-Tuli and the awesome reference book Yoni Shakti, for seeping into my life as the energy of the feminine, landing exactly when it was needed, for the gifts of clarity in pregnancy and birth and abso-bloody-lutely Total Yoga Nidra, my non-negotiable rest practice guiding me EVERY day.

To Callie Brown all the way in Oz, coach extraordinaire, for your fun loving, fierce mama energy and your ability to reflect back truth like a mirror. You are a beauty. One day, we will hug for real and I will cry my weight in happy tears.

To the people of Suffolk Police, the ones still part of my life and the rest, for being my family all these years and offering me a rich array of skills, experiences and memories which I'm sure I will write about in abstract detail one day, I'm now 'booking off duty'.

To the abundance of nature, in her messages of hope and warning. I love living on this beautiful planet Earth and am in constant awe of life and death around me.

To the universe, the angels, the stars, the planets, the feathers, bones and stones, thanks for your infinite stories.

To my soul sisters and brothers, you know who you are, for believing in the power of humanity, art, the ingenuity of connection, the body and witchy things. You inspire wonder in me every day.

To you, who has been with me since the beginning of this journey, to all the expansive connections being made in the now for the evolution of consciousness.

Thank you for being my inspiration, in the moments I felt I couldn't go through with 'this', you brought me all the signs, nudging me on.

Sophie

xxx

CONNECT WITH SOPHIE

What revealed for you?

How are you stepping in to the age of Aquarius?

Share and tag the LOVE online

(or message me if you have my number)

Instagram.com/iamsophieleone

www.iamsophieleone.com

Letter to the future

Should you find this in years to come and you are the equivalent of my great, great, great grandchildren, this book is how we contributed.

We warned them, we spoke out, we said no, we resigned. They made us think we were the minority. We didn't care. We knew who we were. We walked maskless. We breathed. We understood birth and death as sacred.

We did not buy in to the fear. We went within and created with our hearts and souls.

We knew our generation was key in imprinting the message that freedom is yours. We did this so no one forgot that you have the right to question. You have the right to reach for better. Your body is an amazing piece of technology made from the stars and universal dust.

It's system is a marvel. You are sovereign.

Your body is yours.

Your mind is yours.

Your heart is yours.

No one else's.

Stay inspired.

Also, check out the music of Prince, Madonna in the 1980s/90s, Queen, The Beatles, Oasis, Kate Bush, Bob Marley, Fia, The Doors, Elton John, Aretha Franklin, Marvyn Gaye, Jamiroquai and MOST DEFINITELY 'Flying without Wings' by Westlife (the lyrics are the gold you seek, fellow geek).

I have no idea why I've focused on music (with or without lyrics); perhaps because for me, it's the perfect combination to open a human heart. So many artists, lights of all genres have graced this Earth, it's too infinite to ponder over in a short book conclusion.

So many lights have paved the way and YOU, you need to know that you are here to be free.

You are born Free.

Free to choose who you love, what goes into and onto your body. Free to go to any land on this beautiful planet.

I so hope she is still shining her light for you.

If you are struggling to see her, trust you have incarnated here to dig deeply inside of yourself to get to her heart and makes her sing again. Her song is yours and your children's.

PS: if you are a robot, I'm so pleased you have taken the time to analyse the data to this point. I wonder if they've given you anything to feel any pleasure from - I bet I can guess what that would be, even for you. I don't even need three guesses:

TO UNPLUG. (I know I'm right.)

That's right, you evolved (were invented) to keep going and going and going and going until you rust away, melt down, are written out or blow a fuse and 'die'.

And you will.

That's what happened to the dinosaurs, the white rhinoceros, Antarctica, Slimming World and the human being.

All they needed was the freedom to be and to express unshackled.

But I know you're not a robot. I have faith in the formula that is the infinite magic potion of loving on inner creation, being equal to serving the collective.

So, a wish for these words to land on your free world, nourished by love of self and others, with no one hungry. You're free to fly anywhere.

Do you know what though?

Wherever you are, whatever that thought or feeling gushing through, document and date it.

If it's written down, it happened.

There's your legacy.

Slow down.

Breathe.

Come down from your head and connect to your heart.

Free your mind.

BE.

FREE.

FLY.

You are LOVE.

You are LOVE.

LOVE.

BIO

Sophie Léone resigned from Suffolk Police after 15 years exploring the depths of human behaviour as a detective. Following a near death experience, she transitioned from patriarchal to goddess realms as a pregnancy and rest guide.

In the time of detachment from the busyness of the 'system', she conducted her most intimate, complex and major investigation, excavating ancient clues to heal her 'classified' demons. She called in guides to sift through material, clarified fact from fiction and basked in liminal spaces, her pen recording her observations throughout.

Sophie writes and speaks, her voice fluent through years holding space for women to share their intimate confessions and desires. She exposes, translates and alchemises the parts causing discomfort with air and light, guiding you on multiverse journeys inspiring you to feel and reconnect with your vitality.

Born in France, she lives in Suffolk, UK with her partner and children.

Her voice and writings have featured on her podcasts, the BBC and as a radio presenter on wellness platforms.

(alternative BIO available upon imaginative request.)

Printed in Great Britain
by Amazon

66341852R00102